ISBN 978-1-332-83187-6
PIBN 10150624

This book is a reproduction of an important historical work. Forgotten Books uses
state-of-the-art technology to digitally reconstruct the work, preserving the original format
whilst repairing imperfections present in the aged copy. In rare cases, an imperfection in
the original, such as a blemish or missing page, may be replicated in our edition. We do,
however, repair the vast majority of imperfections successfully; any imperfections that
remain are intentionally left to preserve the state of such historical works.

1 MONTH OF
FREE
READING

at
www.ForgottenBooks.com

By purchasing this book you are eligible for one month membership to ForgottenBooks.com, giving you unlimited access to our entire collection of over 700,000 titles via our web site and mobile apps.

To claim your free month visit:
www.forgottenbooks.com/free150624

English
Français
Deutsche
Italiano
Español
Português

www.forgottenbooks.com

Mythology Photography **Fiction**
Fishing Christianity **Art** Cooking
Essays Buddhism Freemasonry
Medicine **Biology** Music **Ancient
Egypt** Evolution Carpentry Physics
Dance Geology **Mathematics** Fitness
Shakespeare **Folklore** Yoga Marketing
Confidence Immortality Biographies
Poetry **Psychology** Witchcraft
Electronics Chemistry History **Law**
Accounting **Philosophy** Anthropology
Alchemy Drama Quantum Mechanics
Atheism Sexual Health **Ancient History**
Entrepreneurship Languages Sport
Paleontology Needlework Islam
Metaphysics Investment Archaeology
Parenting Statistics Criminology
Motivational

n the Supreme Court of the United States

OCTOBER TERM, 1922.

COMMONWEALTH OF MASSACHUSETTES,

Plaintiff

v.

ANDREW W. MELLON, Secretary of the Treasury, et al.,

Defendants.

---

ief on behalf of the Association of Land-Grant Colleges, as amicus curiae, in Support of Motion to Dismiss Bill of Complaint.

CHARLES K. BURDICK,
of Counsel.

INDEX

TABLE OF CASES

IN THE SUPREME COURT OF THE UNITED STATES

OCTOBER TERM, 1922

COMMONWEALTH OF MASSACHUSETTS,
Plaintiff,

vs.

ANDREW W. MELLON, Secretary of the Treasury; GRACE ABBOTT, Chief of the Children's Bureau of the Department of Labor; HUGH S. CUMMING, Surgeon- General of the Public Health Service; JOHN J. TIGERT, Commissioner of Education,

Defendants

No. 24, Original

Brief on behalf of the Association of Land-Grant Colleges as amicus curiae in support of the motion to dismiss the bill of complaint.

This brief is filed in support of the motion to dismiss the bill of complaint, upon the ground that it does not present justiciable questions and that it is without equity.

The Association of Land-Grant Colleges, though not directly interested in the Sheppard-Towner Act, is vitally interested in the constitutional questions involved in this suit brought to test the validity of that Act, since the members of this Association are beneficiaries to a very large extent under various federal statutes having features attacked as unconstitutional by the commonwealth of Massachusetts in its complaint.

The bill of complaint is directed against the alleged unconstitutionality of the so-called Sheppard-Towner Act, being "An Act for the promotion of the welfare and hygiene of maternity and infancy and for other purposes". (Act of Nov. 23, 1921.) The suit is brought as one in equity under the Constitution and laws of the United States by the State of Massachusetts to restrain defendants from exercising the powers conferred and from performing the duties imposed by the Sheppard-Towner Act, on the ground that that Act is unconstitutional and void. It appears from the bill of comclaint that the federal legislation in question is attacked on two general grounds: (a) that Congress cannot constitutionally appropriate money raised by federal taxation to be used by the States for the purpose designated in the Statute, and (b) that the legislation in question constitutes an unconstitutional infringement of the police power, reserved by the Constitution to the individual States.

We present the following points:

First. The Congress of the United States has a constitutional right to levy taxes and to appropriate funds raised by taxation for the general welfare of the United States.

Second. In the interest of the general welfare Congress may provide for the expenditure by the several States of funds raised by federal taxation.

Third. The purposes for which funds are appropriated in the Sheppard-Towner Act, and the provisions therein contained for the administration of those funds by the States are constitutional.

Fourth. The question of usurpation by the federal government of the governmental powers reserved to the States is a political question which is not within the jurisdiction of the Supreme Court of the United States.

Fifth. Federal legislation, which should provide for the grant of financial aid to States upon condition of their abdication or surrender of essential governmental powers, would not constitute a usurpation by Congress of the governmental powers reserved to the States.

Sixth. An abdication or surrender by state legislation of state governmental powers as a term of acceptance of federal aid would at most be a breach of the state constitution. Furthermore, since Massachusetts has not accepted the offer made in the Sheppard-Towner Act there can have been no surrender at all on her part.

Seventh. The Sheppard-Towner Act does not call for the abdication or surrender by a State of any essential governmental power as a condition of the receipt of the federal aid therein provided for.

ARGUMENT.

FIRST: The Congress of the United States has a constitutional right to levy taxes and to appropriate funds raised by taxation for the general welfare of the United States.

The government of the United States is one of limited powers, for the Tenth Amendment declares that, "The powers not delegated to the United States by the Constitution nor prohibited to the States, are reserved to the States respectively or to the people." The power of taxation is expressly granted to the national government. The Constitution declares that, "The Congress shall have power: to lay and collect taxes, duties and excises, to pay the debts and provide for the common defense and general welfare of the United States." (Art. I, Sec. 8, par. 1.)

At the time of its promulgation, the Constitution was attacked on the ground, among others, that the last clause of the paragraph just quoted gave to Congress unlimited power to *legislate* for the common defense and for the general welfare.

This argument Madison effectively refuted in the Federalist (No. 41), pointing out that the last clause of that paragraph is a qualification upon the taxing power, and not a general grant of legislative power. This interpretation has been universally accepted.

On the other hand, any suggestion that the federal powers of taxation, and of appropriation of funds raised by taxation, are confined to the furtherance of the exercise of other enumerated powers is clearly untenable. Hamilton in 1791, in his Report on Manufactures, stated it as his clear opinion that the phrase "general welfare" "is as comprehensive as any that could have been used," and that "there seems no reason to doubt that whatever concerns the general interests of learning, of agriculture, of manufactures, and of commerce, are within the sphere of the national councils as far as regards an application of money. The only qualification of the generality of the phrase in question which seems to be admissible is this: that the object to which an appropriation of money is to be made must be general and not local,—its operation extending in fact, or by possibility throughout the Union, and not being confined to a particular spot."

President Monroe, in an elaborate and very cogent paper entitled "Views of the President of the United States on the subject of Internal Improvements," submitted with his veto in 1822 of the Cumberland Road Bill, took the same view. He said in part:

"The powers specially granted to Congress are what are called the enumerated powers, and are numbered in the order in which they stand, among which that contained in the first clause holds the first place in point of importance. * * * A power to lay and collect taxes, duties, imposts, and excises subjects to the call of Congress every branch of the public revenue, internal and external, and the addition to pay the debts and provide for the common defense and general welfare gives the right of applying the money raised—that is, of appropriating it to the purposes specified according to a proper construction of the terms. Hence it follows that it is the first part of the clause only which gives a power which affects in any manner the power remaining to the States, as the power to raise money from the people, whether it be taxes, duties, imposts, or excises, though concurrent in the States as to taxes and excises, must necessarily do.

"But the use or application of the money after it is raised is a power altogether of a different character. It imposes no burden on the people, nor can it act on them in a sense to take power from the States or in any sense in which power can be controverted, or become a question between the two Governments. The application of money raised under a lawful power is a right or grant which may be abused. It may be applied partially among the States, or to improper purposes in our foreign and domestic concerns; but still it is a power not felt in the sense of other power, since the only complaint which any State can make of such partiality and abuse is that some other State or States have obtained greater benefit from the application than by a just rule of apportionment they were entitled to.

****

"With this construction all the other enumerated grants, and indeed, all the grants of power contained in the Constitution, have their full operation and effect. They all stand well together, fulfilling the great purposes intended by them. Under it we behold a great scheme consistent in all its parts, a Government instituted for national purposes, vested with adequate powers for those purposes, commencing with the most important of all, that of the revenue, and proceeding in regular order to the others with which it was deemed proper to endow it, all, too, drawn with the utmost circumspection and care".

President Jackson, in his veto in 1830 of the Maysville Turnpike Bill, expressed the same opinion of the Constitutional provision. This is the view taken generally by writers on the Constitution. (Story on the Constitution (5th ed.) sec. 923; Willoughby on the Constitution, pp. 589-592; Watson on the Constitution, pp. 390-398; Burdick, The Law of the American Constitution, sec. 77.)

This view is obviously correct. Section 8 of Article I of the Constitution contains, in seventeen separate clauses or paragraphs, certain distinct grants of power, and in the eighteenth paragraph the power, "To make all laws which shall be necessary and proper for carrying into execution the foregoing powers, and all other powers vested by the Constitution in the government of the United States, or in any department or officer thereof." It is thus apparent from the text of this section, that the power to "lay and collect taxes, duties, imposts and excises", in paragraph one, is as distinct from the other powers as is each one of them distinct from the others, and that federal taxation and appropriations do not have to be confined to the furtherance of one of the other enumerated powers, but may be enacted for any purpose which fairly comes within the clause "to pay the debts and provide for the common defense and general welfare of the United States".

Up to the present time, there has been no inclination to ask for a judicial determination of the scope of congressional power under the welfare clause contained in the grant of the taxing power. However, in *United States* v. *Realty Company* (1896) 163 U.S. 427, an attack was made upon an appropriation by Congress for the payment of claims not legal in character, but based merely upon moral or honorary considerations. The Court said (p. 440): "It is unnecessary to hold here that Congress has the power to appropriate the public money in the treasury to any purpose whatever which it may choose to say is in payment of a debt, or for purposes of the general welfare. A decision of that question may be postponed until it arises." But the Court did hold that "debts", for which Congress may lay taxes and appropriate national funds, include such claims as were provided for by the legislation in question, and declared that the decision of Congress "recognizing such a claim and appropriating money for its payment can rarely, if ever, be the subject of review by the judicial branch of the government."

If such almost conclusive effect is given to congressional determination of what is a "debt" owed by the United States, it is clear that the determination by Congress that a given appropriation constitutes a provision for the "public welfare," will be accepted by the Supreme Court unless it is palpably and unmistakeably without any foundation or justification in fact. This is the attitude taken by the Supreme Court with regard to the exercise by the States of their police power for the general welfare of their inhabitants (*Noble State Bank* v. *Haskell* (1911) 219 U. S. 104, 111; *Price* v. *Illinois* (1915) 238 U. S. 446, 452), and with regard to the exercise by the United States of its similar power over the District of Columbia (*Block* v. *Hirsh* (1921) 256 U. S. 135, 154). (See also the very instructive article by R. E. Cushman, "The Social and Economic Interpretation of the 14th Amendment", 20 Mich. L. R. 735.)

After the Revolution vast tracts of western lands claimed by different States were ceded to the federal government in response to a "resolve" passed by Congress that the territory ceded would be disposed of for the common benefit of the United States, and would eventually be erected into States. (Curtis' History of the Constitution, Vol. I, pp. 131-138, 291-301; Story on the Constitution (5th ed.) sec. 1316; Burdick, The Law of the American Constitution, sec. 100.) It seems clear that the territories procured from France and Spain by purchase with funds of the United States obtained from taxes paid by the people of the United States were equally held by the United States subject to the duty to dispose of them for the common benefit.

Extensive appropriations of land have been made by Congress to the States and to subdivisions of the States for the benefit of education from the very earliest days. The constitutionality of these appropriations seems never to have been questioned, but, on the other hand, has been, by implication, repeatedly assumed, for the provisions of the statutes have been interpreted and applied by the Supreme Court in a very large number of cases. (*Campbell* v. *Doe* (1851) 13 Howard

244; *Haire* v. *Rice* (1907) 204 U. S. 291; *California* v. *Desert W., O. & I. Co.* (1917) 243 U. S. 415; and cases cited in Digest Supreme Court Reports, pp. 4823-4829.) In *Wyoming* v. *Irvine* (1907) 206 U. S. 278, the Morrill Act (Act of July 2, 1862, 12 Stats. 503), the first nation-wide appropriation of land to the purposes of education, was interpreted by the Supreme Court without any suggestion that its constitutionality was questionable.   This Morrill Act was followed in 1890 by the so-called Second Morrill Act (Act of Aug. 30, 1890, 26 Stats. 417), by which further appropriations of public lands were made to educational purposes, and a few years earlier by the Hatch Act (Act of March 2, 1887, 24 Stats. 440), by which proceeds of public lands were appropriated to the same purposes.

To be sure these acts appropriate public lands or their proceeds, and so are not identical with federal legislation appropriating money raised by taxation.   But if public lands can be only used for the common benefit, the uses to which they have without question been put over a long period of years would seem to be persuasive as to what should be considered constitutional in the way of appropriation of federal funds raised by taxation for the "general welfare." Common benefit and general welfare would seem to be terms of quite identical significance.   And certainly Congress has taken this view, for in the Adams Act (Act of March 16, 1908, 34 Stats. 63), the Smith-Lever Act (Act of May 8, 1914, 38 Stats. 372), and the Smith-Hughes Act (Act of Feb. 23, 1917, 39 Stats. 929) it has followed its appropriations of public lands and their proceeds with appropriations of large sums of money raised by general taxation for the purpose of the advancement of education throughout the country.

SECOND: In the interest of the general welfare Congress may provide for the expenditure by the several States of funds raised by federal taxation.

It is universally recognized as a fundamental principal of American constitutional law that the legislative branch of the government cannot delegate its essential legislative functions

to any other agency. This results from the clear declaration
in our constitutions, both federal and state, that all legislative
power shall vest in the law-making bodies which are thereby
created. This does not mean that Congress cannot delegate
any of the powers which it has a right to exercise. A distinction is drawn between those powers which are essentially
legislative, and those which are not. As said by Chief Justice
Marshall (*Wayman* v. *Southard*, (1825) 10 Wheat. 1, 42):

> "It will not be contended that Congress can delegate
> to the courts, or to any other tribunal powers which are
> strictly or exclusively legislative. But Congress may
> certainly delegate to others powers which the legislature
> may rightfully exercise itself."

In a later case it is said (*Field* v. *Clark* (1892) 143 U. S.
649, 693):

> "The true distinction * * * is between the delegation
> of power to make the law, which necessarily involves a
> discretion as to what it shall be, and conferring author-
> ity or discretion as to its execution, to be exercised
> under and in pursuance of the law. The first cannot be
> done; to the latter no valid objection can be made."

Many cases of judicial recognition of this distinction might
be collected, of which perhaps the most striking are those recognizing the validity of the delegation to the Interstate Commerce Commission of the power to fix rates (*Interstate Commerce Comm.* v. *Illinois* (1910) 215 U. S. 452; *Interstate Commerce Comm.* v. *Chicago R. I. and* P. *Ry. Co.* (1910) 218 U. S.
88), and the delegation to the President of the power to determine whether the privilege of free introduction of certain
commodities should be suspended. (*Field* v. *Clark* (1892) 143
U. S. 649.)

It is obvious that the delegation by Congress to the States
of the exercise of its essential legislative powers would be as
unconstitutional as a similar delegation to the executive or
judicial branch of the federal government. (*Cooley* v. *Port*

Wardens of Philadelphia (1851) 12 How. 299, 318; *In re Rohrer* (1891) 140 U. S. 545, 560.) But in the case last cited the court suggested (pp. 561 and 562), by way of dictum, that, by analogy to local option laws, Congress might make a law which would leave to the States "to determine some fact or state of things, upon which the action of the law may depend." In other cases the Supreme Court of the United States has directly recognized the right of Congress, when legislating upon a subject within its exclusive jurisdiction, to delegate to the state legislatures the power to legislate with regard to designated details. In *Hanover National Bank* v. *Moyses* (1902) 186 U. S. 181, the court upheld the provision of the National Bankruptcy Act which gives effect to such exemptions as may be prescribed by the laws of the State of domicile in force at the time of filing the petition in bankruptcy. And in *Butte City Water Company* v. *Baker* (1905) 196 U. S. 119, the court held constitutional a delegation to the state legislatures of the power to regulate the location of mining claims on public lands.

The federal government has also, from the beginning of its history, made use of state agencies in various ways in carrying out the administration of its laws. From the first naturalization statute in 1790 until the present day Congress has conferred upon state courts the right to naturalize aliens, and this delegation of power to state courts has been held constitutional. (*Holmgren* v. *United States* (1910) 217 U. S. 509.) When slavery still existed in this country it was held that Congress, in enforcing the constitutional provision for the return of fugitive slaves, might constitutionally confer upon state officers authority to act for the federal government. (*Prigg* v. *Pennsylvania* (1842) 16 Pet. 539.) Congress may delegate to state courts the power to determine the amount of compensation to be paid by the United States for private property taken under its power of eminent domain. (*United States* v. *Jones* (1883) 109 U. S. 513.) Congress may also give to state courts jurisdiction of suits for the enforcement of the federal revenue laws (*Kentucky* v. *Dennsion* (1860) 24 How. 66, 108, 109), and may authorize state officers to arrest persons for federal offenses. (*Robertson* v. *Baldwin* (1897) 165 U. S. 275.)

In all of the "Federal Aid" legislation in support of nation-wide education, considered in Part One of this brief, from the Morrill Act in 1862 to the Smith-Hughes Act in 1917, the States have been appointed agents or trustees to administer the lands or the funds according to the terms of the grants. These grants have been accepted and administered by the States without question.

THIRD: The purposes for which funds are appropriated in the Sheppard-Towner Act, and the provisions therein contained for the administration of those funds by the States are constitutional.

The so-called Sheppard-Towner Act, being "An Act for the promotion of the welfare and hygiene of maternity and infancy and for other purposes" (Act of Nov. 23, 1921), appropriates certain sums therein named "to be paid to the several States for the purpose of cooperating with them in promoting the welfare and hygiene of maternity and infancy." (Sec. 1.)

It is submitted that the money raised by federal taxation is appropriated by this legislation to the "general welfare of the United States." That the welfare of any community will be advanced by promoting the "welfare and hygiene of maternity and infancy" would seem to need no argument. The generality of the legislation fully meets the test suggested by Hamiliton—a test which seems eminently sound: "that the the object to which an appropriation of money is to be made must be general and not local,—its operation extending in fact, or by possibility, throughout the Union, and not being confined to a particular spot" (Report on Manufactures, 1791), since by the terms of the statute it is to become operative in each State upon the acceptance of its terms by the state legislature. (Sec. 4.) The fact that some States may accept the federal aid which is offered while others may fail to do so does not affect the generality or uniformity of the federal legislation. It is uniform in its terms. The fact that various state action may prevent its being uniform in operation does not prove that in it there is any lack of uniformity. (*Clark Distilling Company* v. *Western Maryland Railway Co.* (1917) 242 U. S. 311, 326, 327.)

The States by force of their acceptance of the terms of the Act are to become agents or trustees for the administration of the funds appropriated by Congress. For this purpose the state legislatures are to create or designate state agencies which are to formulate plans for the administration of the federal funds. (Secs. 4 and 8.) Here is clearly no unconstitutional delegation by Congress of essential legislative powers. As has been pointed out in Part Two of this brief, when Congress has declared the purposes which are to be attained, it may delegate the execution of those purposes and the formulation of regulations for their execution. As has also been pointed out, Congress may authorize the States to act for the federal government, and may delegate to the States the formulation of rules for carrying out the details of federal legislation. This was strongly intimated *In re Rohrer* (1891) 140 U. S. 545, 560, and expressly decided in *Hanover National Bank* v. *Moyses* (1902) 186 U. S. 181, and in *Butte City Water Company* v. *Baker* (1905) 196 U. S. 119, which are discussed in Part Two of this brief together with other cases where the States have been employed to act for the federal government. As has also been pointed out, the federal government has from the beginning of our national history appropriated land or money for the advancement of education, and has placed the administration of such land or money in the hands of the States or of their political subdivisions.

It may be that "Federal Aid" legislation is open to criticism on the ground that part of the money derived by federal taxation from the States where there is greater aggregation of wealth is distributed among States where there is less wealth. Some persons may, perhaps, doubt whether this is wise, and may urge that the resources of the States, respectively, should not be applied directly for the benefit of the inhabitants of other States. Other persons may believe that the federal government should look to the welfare of the whole country without regard to state lines. In view of the language of the Constitution, these would seem to be matters for the consideration of Congress in the exercise of its discretion as to how the general welfare can best be advanced, and not for the consideration of the Court in the determination of the constitutionality of such taxation and appropriation as is here under discussion.

FOURTH: The question of usurpation by the federal government of the governmental powers reserved to the States is a political question which is not within the jurisdiction of the Supreme Court of the United States.

It is asserted in the bill of complaint that the "Sheppard-Towner Act is a usurpation of a power not granted to Congress by the Constitution and an attempted exercise of the power of local self-government reserved to the States by the Tenth Amendment; * * * that Congress cannot assume and state legislature cannot yield the powers reserved to the States by the Tenth Amendment." (p. 8.) It appears that the State of Massachusetts is complaining that the government of the United States is usurping certain political, governmental powers reserved to the States by the Tenth Amendment to the Constitution of the United States, and that this State wishes to have this Court determine a purely political controversy between it and the government of the United States, in which no personal or property rights are involved.

An administrative officer of the United States may be enjoined from doing acts injurious to persons or to property rights under cover of unconstitutional legislation (*Allen* v. *Baltimore and Ohio Railway Company* (1884) 114 U. S. 311; *Ex parte Young* (1908) 209 U. S. 123; *Philadelphia Company* v. *Stimson* (1912) 223 U. S. 605), but in *Georgia* v. *Stanton* (1867) 6 Wall. 50, the Supreme Court held that a State could not maintain an action against the Secretary of War to restrain the execution of the Reconstruction Acts, the gravamen of the bill being that the execution of the acts of Congress would destroy the sovereignty of the State by abolishing the existing state government. The court refused to entertain the action on the ground that it called for a judgment with regard to a purely political controversy between the United States and the State of Georgia. The court said:

> "In looking into it, it will be seen that we are called upon to restrain the defendants, who represent the executive authority of the government, from carrying into execution certain acts of Congress, inasmuch as such execution would annul, and totally abolish the existing state government of Georgia, and establish another and different one in its place; in other words, would overthrow and destroy the corporate existence of the State, by depriving it of all the means and instrumentailities whereby its existence might, and, otherwise would be maintained.

> *   *   *   *   *   *   *   *

> "That these matters, both as stated in the body of the bill, and, in the prayers for relief, call for the judgment of the court upon political questions, and upon, rights, not of persons or property, but of a political character, will hardly be denied. For the rights for the protection of which our authority is invoked, are the rights of sovereignty, of political jurisdiction, of government, of corporate existence as a State, with all its constitutional powers and privileges. No case of private rights or private property infringed, or in danger of actual or threatened infringement, is presented by the bill, in a judicial form, for the judgment of the court."

In the case of *Georgia* v. *Stanton* the court relied quite largely upon the earlier case of *Cherokee Nation* v. *Georgia* (1831) 1 Pet. 1, in which the Cherokee Nation sought to restrain the State of Georgia from exercising legislative power over them. The court held that it had no original jurisdiction of the case because the Cherokee Nation was not a foreign nation within the meaning of the Judiciary Article of the Constitution; but the judges also declared that the controversy

with regard to the legislative control of the Indian Nation by
the State of Georgia was purely political, and, therefore, not
a proper one for the court to entertain. See also *Wisconsin
v. Pelican Insurance Company* (1888) 127 U. S. 265, 296.

It is true that two of the suits involving the constitutionality of the Eighteenth Amendment, reported under the title
of the *National Prohibition Cases* (1920) 253 U. S. 350, were
brought by the States of Rhode Island and New Jersey. In
the other suits brought by private persons property rights
were involved. The bills brought by the States of Rhode
Island and New Jersey were dismissed. No opinion was written
for the court, and the question of jurisdiction was, therefore
not discussed. The court simply announced certain con-
clusions as to the validity of the Eighteenth Amendment, and
as to its meaning. The *National Prohibition Cases* cannot,
therefore, be said to affect the authority of the considered
opinions in *Cherokee Nation* v. *Georgia* and *Georgia* v. *Stanton*.

**FIFTH: Federal legislation, which should provide for the
grant of financial aid to States upon condition of their adbi-
cation or surrender of essential governmental powers, would
not constitute a usurpation by Congress of the governmental
powers reserved to the States.**

The Tenth Amendment of the Constitution of the United
States reserves to the States all of the powers of government
possessed by them at the time of the Constitution's adoption
and not by that instrument prohibited to them or transferred
to the national government. Thus the States have generally
the power to take money by taxation, or property by eminent
domain for public use, and to restrict the activity of in-
dividuals under the police power for the protection of the
health, safety, morals and general welfare of the community.
The federal government may not constitutionally usurp the
functions of the state governments either in the exercise of its
power over interstate commerce (*Hammer* v. *Dagenhart*
(1918) 247 U. S. 251), or in the exercise of its taxing power

(*Bailey* v. *Drexel Furniture Company* (1922) 42 Sup. Ct. R. 449), though it may and does very vitally affect the internal affairs of the States in the course of the exercise of the powers granted to it. (*Bank* v. *Fenno* (1869) 8 Wallace 533, a prohibitive tax on notes of state banks; *Railroad Comm. of Wis.* v. *Ohio B. & O. R. Co.* (1922) 42 Sup. Ct. R. 232; *New York* v. *United States* (1922) 42 Sup. Ct. R. 239, regulation of intrastate rates where they affect interstate commerce; *McDermott* v. *Wisconsin* (1913) 228 U. S. 115, 128, prohibition of the transportation from State to State of foods and drugs which do not conform to standards established by federal legislation.)

In the bill of complaint, the Sheppard-Towner Act is attacked as unconstitutional on the grounds that it is an infringement by Congress of the power of local self-government reserved to the States by the Constitution, because of the conditions which must be met by any State which chooses to accept the benefits of the law.

Let us suppose, for the sake of the argument, that federal legislation appropriating money or conveying public land to the use of the States for educational or other welfare purposes makes the receipt of such money or land by a State conditional upon the agreement by the State not to exercise some reserved governmental power, or to delegate its exercise to the government of the United States. Would such federal legislation of itself be unconstitutional? It would constitute of itself no infringement upon the sphere of the government of any State. It would be wholly ineffective with regard to any State until accepted by that State. Such legislation would not, then, constitute a usurpation by the government of the United States of the governmental powers reserved by the Federal Constitution to the States.

If, then, it should appear (which we shall show later is not the case) that the Sheppard-Towner Act requires, upon the acceptance by a State of its benefits, that the State shall agree not to exercise some reserved governmental powers, or shall delegate their exercise to the government of the United States, this federal legislation would not thereby be made unconstitutional as a usurpation of State powers.

SIXTH: An abdication or surrender by state legislation of state governmental powers as a term of acceptance of federal aid would at most be a breach of the state constitution. Furthermore, since Massachusetts has not accepted the offer made in the Sheppard-Towner Act there can have been no surrender at all on her part.

If a State in its legislative acceptance of a grant of land or of money from the federal government should agree not to exercise some reserved governmental power, or to delegate its exercise to the government of the United States, this would seem not to contravene any provision of the Constitution of the United States, and so would seem to raise no question for the decision of the federal courts. The Tenth Amendment reserves certain powers to the States, but there is no provision in the federal constitution which would prevent the delegation by a state legislature of its powers to Congress, or an agreement by a State not to exercise a governmental power.

State courts have held that under their *state* constitutions the legislatures of the States are forbidden to delegate their lawmaking functions to the legislatures of other States or to Congress, as, for instance, when they attempt to declare that future legislation of such bodies shall be the law of their States. (*Dowling* v. *Lancashire* (1896) 92 Wis. 63; *In re Opinion of Justices* (Mass., 1921) 133 N. E. 453. But see *People* v. *Phila. Fire Assoc.* (1883) 92 N. Y. 311.) But this is on the ground that the *state* constitutions by granting lawmaking power to the state legislatures require by implication that they alone shall exercise that power. Any attempt at delegation by them is, then, at most an infringement of the state and not of the federal constitution.

Similarly it is held that an agreement by a state legislature not to exercise certain of its essential legislative functions conflicts with the grant to the legislature of law-making power contained in the *state* constitution. This is true of the State's power of eminent domain (*Pennsylvania Hospital* v. *Philadelphia* (1917) 246 U. S. 20), and generally of its police powers (*Fertilizer Co.* v. *Hyde Park* (1878) 97 U. S. 659; *Beer Co.* v. *Massachusetts* (1877) 97 U. S. 25; *Chicago and A. R.R. Co.* v. *Tranbarger* (1915) 236 U. S. 67,—though not of its power to fix rates, *Freeport Water Co.* v. *Freeport* (1901) 180 U. S. 587; *Vicksburg* v. *Vicksburg W. W. Co.* (1906) 206 U. S. 496), but it is held not to be true of its taxing power (*New Jersey* v. *Wilson* (1812) 7 Cranch 164; *New Orleans* v. *Houston* (1886) 119 U. S. 265). The claim, then, that such an attempted surrender is void would not of itself raise a question under the Constitution of the United States so as to give a federal court jurisdiction. A federal question only arises, when, the State having made such a surrender in the form of a contract, the other party to the contract seeks the protection of the provision of the Federal Constitution which forbids States to impair the obligation of contracts. If such a contract is valid the federal courts will enforce it. But if it is void because the state legislature has acted contrary to the limitations implied in the state constitution, the federal courts will not enforce it. (See the cases above cited.)

But in fact the question of the effect of an attempt by a State to abdicate or surrender State governmental powers as a term of acceptance of federal aid cannot arise in this case at all, since the Massachussets legislature has failed to accept the offer made by the federal government in the Sheppard-Towner Act, and, therefore, has clearly surrendered no governmental powers as a condition to the receipt of aid under that act.

SEVENTH: The Sheppard-Towner Act does not call for the abdication or surrender by a State of any essential governmental power as a condition of the receipt of the federal aid therein provided for.

The requirements exacted of the States as conditions of the receipt of federal aid under the Sheppard-Towner Act are as follows:

1. Management of federal funds.

    (a) The money granted to the States to be used for "promoting the welfare and hygiene of maternity and infancy" (Sec. 1); and not to be used for land, buildings or equipment. (Sec. 12.)

    (b) A state agency to be designated to cooperate with the federal government. (Sec. 4.)

    (c) Reports of expenditures and work done to be made to a federal agency. (Sec. 11.)

2. The State to contribute certain sums to be used in connection with the federal funds. (Sec. 2.)

3. The state agency to submit to a federal agency plans for the work to be done, which it is the duty of the federal agency to approve if ' in conformity with the provisions of this Act and reasonably appropriate and adequate to carry out its purposes'. (Sec. 8.) Apportionment to a State of federal funds to be made only if plans have been submitted to a federal agency and approved, and not to be made if the federal agency upon a report made by the state agency determines that federal funds have been improperly expended, but such determination can be reached only after a hearing, and is subject to review by the President. (Secs. 10 and 11).

4. Money appropriated by the State for cooperation with the federal government not to be used for maternity or infancy pensions, stipends or gratuities. (Sec. 12.)

5. There is a proviso in Section 8, "That the plans of the States under this act shall provide that no official, or agent, or representative in carrying out the provisions of this Act shall enter any home or take charge of any child over the objections of the parents, or either of them, or the person standing in loco parentis or having custody of such child."

The provisions put in Group One clearly involve no surrender of governmental powers. They are merely proper and reasonable engagements entered into by the State as trustee of a fund to use the fund as designated by the donor, and to report with regard to its trusteeship. This group needs no further comment. That a State may make contracts which are binding upon it (*Dartmouth College* v. *Woodward* (1819) 4 Wheaton 518), and that a grant by the United States to a State, accepted by it upon certain conditions named, is such a contract (*McGehee* v. *Mathis* (1866) 4 Wallace 143, 155) are well established propositions.

It is quite as clear that the provisions (numbered 2 above) to which the State may agree, for the appropriation of state funds constitutes no surrender of governmental powers. Such an agreement is simply to exercise for a public purpose the governmental powers of raising money and of appropriating it. This has been repeatedly done by the federal government by treaty and supplementary legislation, as when the United States purchased the Louisiana Territory, Florida and the Virgin Islands. Such an agreement between Virginia and West Virginia has been enforced by the Supreme Court of the United States. (*Virginia* v. *West Virginia* (1915) 238 U. S. 202, (1916) 241 U. S. 531, (1918) 246 U. S. 565.) There seems no ground to doubt the constitutionality of such an agreement entered into between the United States and a State.

The provisions which are put in Group Three, above, are obviously introduced into the Act so that the federal government may reserve a certain amount of control over the administration of this Act by the state agencies. Yet such control is only for the purpose of assuring the fulfillment of the objects of the Act in so far as it has been accepted by the States. It is true that the judges of the question whether the objects of the Act are being fulfilled are in the first place certain administrative officers of the United States, and upon appeal, upon the question of proper past expenditures, the President. But here is no surrender by a State of essential governmental power. By accepting the offer of the federal government it agrees to administer a trust according to its terms, and if its agents do not so administer it, it forfeits the right to the federal aid. But the right of the State to legislate and to administer its laws is in no way curtailed; and there is nothing to prevent it from at any time withdrawing its consent, and surrendering the benefits of the Act.

The term of the Sheppard-Towner Act, put under the fourth subheading above, clearly surrenders no essential governmental power. The State accepting that act may create maternity and infancy pensions if it so desires—it merely makes an agreement as to how a certain sum of money is to be used; the State in response to an offer of the federal government chooses to declare how it will spend a certain amount of the public funds.

By accepting the provision of the Sheppard-Towner Act, put under the fifth subhead above, the State would seem to agree to a certain restriction upon the exercise of its police powers, but, even with regard to the entering of homes and the taking of children there dealt with, the restriction is not general, but applies only to the administration of the Act. The State may still exercise any power which it inherently has, for the protection of the welfare of mothers and children, to enter homes and take children under any legislation which it may enact, which is not for the carrying out of the federal act. It seems clear, therefore, that this is not such a surrender of a police power as would constitute a violation by a state legislature of the implied limitations placed upon it by the state constitution.

It may be that persons may differ as to the wisdom and advantage of federal grants of aid to the States, which are made upon conditions which the States must fulfill in order to take advantage of the grants. It may be contended that such legislation tends to undue centralization of power, at the expense of an unfettered control of intrastate affairs, which should be exercised by the States themselves. But, unless the legislation is clearly unconstitutional, such considerations are for the legislature and not for the court.

Courts may disapprove of the policy of legislation, and may yet be satisfied of its constitutionality. Questions involving the wisdom or policy of legislation are essentially questions for the law-makers and not for the judiciary.

The bill of complaint should be dismissed.

CHARLES K. BURDICK,

As *amicus curiae* and of counsel
for the Association of Land-Grant Colleges.

CPSIA information can be obtained
at www.ICGtesting.com
Printed in the USA
LVHW03s0920060818
586105LV00004B/490/P